CANOEIST'S LITTLE BOOK OF WISDOM

*A Couple Hundred Suggestions, Observations
and Reminders for Canoeists to Read,
Remember and Share.*

By Cliff Jacobson

ICS BOOKS, Inc.
Merrillville, IN

Canoeist's Little Book of Wisdom

Copyright © 1996 by Cliff Jacobson

10 9 8 7 6 5 4 3 2 1

All rights reserved, including the right to reproduce this book or portions thereof
in any form or by any means, electronic or mechanical, including photocopying,
recording, unless authorization is obtained, in writing, from the publisher.

All inquiries should be addressed to ICS Books, Inc, 1370 E. 86th Place, Merrillville, IN 46410

Published by:	**Co-Published in Canada by:**	**Printed in the U.S.A.**
ICS BOOKS, Inc	Vanwell Publishing LTD	All ICS titles are printed on 50% recycled paper fro
1370 E. 86th Place	1 Northrup Crescent	pre-consumer waste. All sheets are processed witho
Merrillville, IN 46410	St. Catharines, Ontario	using acid.
800-541-7323	L2M 6P5	
	800-661-6136	

Library of Congress Cataloging-in-Publication Data

Jacobson, Cliff.
  Canoeist's little book of wisdom / Cliff Jacobson.
    p. cm.
  ISBN 1-57034-040-4
  1. Canoes and canoeing. I. Title.
GV784.J33   1996
797 . 1'22'02--DC20   96-443
                                            CIP

Foreword

When my publisher suggested we title this book "Canoeist's Little Book Of Wisdom," I voiced concern. After all, I argued, I've messed up far too many times to be considered very wise. For example:

Steel River, Ontario, 1987: I wrecked a Kevlar canoe in a rapid I'd successfully paddled five times before. Hood River, Northwest Territories, 1992: capsized in an insignificant rapid. Seal River, Manitoba, 1993: my wife and I came within a yard of paddling over a waterfalls! Caribou River, Manitoba, 1995: a miraculous descent of a technical Class IV rapid I should have portaged around. I could go on, of course, but I see no reason to advertise my imperfections.

The good news is that I have gained humility from my past mistakes. Mostly, I've come to respect the river and to never take for granted a warm sunny day, a tail wind or a bug-free moment. I've learned that if you can't paddle a rapid, you can line it or portage it or drag around it. Indeed, Verlen Kruger made this abundantly clear when he canoed—or rather, "carried"—his solo canoe *up* the Grand Canyon! In his quiet, unassuming way, Verlen proved what expert paddlers have always known—that there's a route around every obstacle, even if it is an unpleasant one.

This book is not about how to paddle canoes or prepare for a wilderness adventure. It is a list of philosophical and practical tips that provide insight into the joy of canoeing quiet ponds and gentle streams and misty lakes and thundering rapids. There is good advice on most everything about canoeing and canoeing gear—and you'll be pleased to know, it's not all mine. Steve Scarborough, Charlie Wilson, Anne Bancroft, Bill Simpson, Bob O'Hara, Dr. Bill Forgey and scores of other paddlers have made their mark on these pages.

You'll discover that the experts don't always agree on what is best. That's because there are "different strokes for different folks." The real wisdom is in knowing what's right for you.

Take time to smell the pines and observe the eagle, touch the rocks and contemplate the wonder of wild places and the magic of canoes.

-Cliff Jacobson

Dedication

To Joe Meinover,
the best special education teacher
I have ever known.
He gives his heart to kids
and makes them realize that
they can achieve their dreams.

Credits

Special thanks to my publisher, Tom Todd, for his help and encouragement.
Thanks also, to the following people who contributed ideas and/or passages to this
book: Anne Bancroft, Ted Bell, Bob Brown, Bob Dannert, Dave Dietrich, Lynn
Dietrich, Dr. Bill Forgey, Darrell Foss, Tom Foster, Mike Link, Bob O'Hara, Sue
Harings, Betty Ketter, the late Harry Roberts, Steve Scarborough, Bill Simpson, Dr.
Tom Schwinghamer, Charlie Wilson.

1. Hold out for the canoe of your dreams, even if you have to make monthly payments.
2. Take time to see the rapid you've just portaged around.
3. Carry some good chocolate bars on every canoe trip.
4. Don't argue about equipment during a caribou migration. Wait till January when the river is frozen.

5. Paddle in time with the sun, not your watch.

6. Carry a knife with a blade that's long enough to reach to the bottom of the peanut butter jar.

7. Messing around with canoes is an appropriate form of entertainment.

8. Store your canoe where you can see it; store your paddle where you can touch it.

9. Prepare a late night supper below a falls on a whisper-quiet trail stove.

10. Paddle an hour with a ten-ounce bent-shaft carbon-fiber racing paddle, then see if you can live without one.

11. A week's worth of paddling instruction is worth a life-time of paddling around.

12. Check your canoe "tie-downs" every time you fill up for gas.

13. Thunder in the morning,
All day storming.
Thunder at night,
Canoeist's delight.

14.   Duct tape may be the canoeist's gray badge of courage, but nylon strapping tape is better for repairing paddles and broken seats.

15.   Kevlar skid plates add weight and ugliness to any canoe. Do-it-yourself patches cut from Kevlar and fiberglass cloth are much lighter and prettier.

16. *"Warm Skin,"* by Aurora, is a *non-greasy* hand cream that acts like an extra pair of gloves. Its udder-balm and aloe formula doesn't make your paddle feel slimy.

– Anne Bancroft

17.   Rain-X® causes rain to bead on windshields. It clears the view for high speed driving, even without windshield wipers. Apply it to your eyeglasses before you paddle in a thunderstorm.

18.   Bring two paddles on every canoe trip. One should be a lightweight model that brings you joy—the other, a sturdier version of the same. Leave at home all ugly sticks you hate to use!

19. Here's how to test the fit of a life jacket:

1. Grasp it by the shoulders and lift up till the fabric jams under your arms. Now, turn your head right and left. Can you see the river?

2. Sit on the floor and draw your arms smartly inward. The vest should not bunch up or cramp your style.

20.   Apply a coat of marine-grade finishing
       oil to the woodwork of your canoe
       several times during the canoeing
       season.

21.   Tighten all the bolts on your canoe at
       least twice a year.

22.   To restore gray, weathered woodwork, sand well, then apply trisodium phosphate (TSP) cleaner, available at hardware stores. Work in with a stiff brush and wear protective gloves. Rinse completely, allow to dry, then sand to silky smoothness.

23. Here's an easy way to repair gouges in the gel-coat of Kevlar and fiberglass canoes:

    1. Pick out the loose shards of gel coat.
    2. Fill the gouge with marine polyester putty or gray auto body putty.
    3. Wet sand smooth, then spray paint to match the hull. Buff with pumice and paste wax.

24. Learn to ferry your canoe out of harm's way. If ducks can do it, you can too!

25. Good canoes appreciate; bad ones depreciate!

26. Don't put good paddles in the trunk of a car where they can rattle around.

27. You'll wreck the finish of a fine paddle if you tie it into a canoe and use it for a portage yoke.

28. Carry a canoe paddle when you rock-hop to scout a rapid. It makes a handy walking stick.

29. Always set bent-shaft paddles on the ground with the blade facing up.

30. Your bent-shaft paddle should be about two inches shorter than your favorite straight paddle.

31.   Never lean a paddle against a tree. Gravity is a sure thing.

32.   If you're canoeing above the treeline, bring along a pair of pruning clippers to snip small twigs for a campfire.

33.   For safety's sake, keep a loud whistle attached to the zipper slider on your life vest. The pea-less "Fox 40" is the clear choice.

34. Don't jeopardize the lives of your kids by equipping them with an adult size life jacket. Read the size/weight recommendation on the label. And, believe it!

35. A skinny teenager may need a life jacket that has more flotation than his fat uncle. Read the label. And believe it!

36.   There are special life jackets for toddlers. Buy one or leave the child at home.

37.   Don't hold your hands too far apart on the canoe paddle. Your lower hand should be positioned about a foot up the shaft—or a distance that's roughly equal to the freeboard of your canoe.

38.   Paddle hard all day in an all-day rain.

39. Paddle your canoe at least once a month every month of the year.

40. If your car has rain gutters, keep it forever!

41. Make three mounds of equipment when you pack for a canoe trip. Place what you <u>need</u> in the first pile, what you <u>may need</u> in the second pile, and what you <u>don't need</u> in the third pile. Take all of the first pile, none of the second pile and one luxury from the last pile.

42. Paddle forth in rain and damp. Spend your sunny days in camp.

43. Think hard before you lend your favorite canoe or paddle to a friend.

44. Never lend a good canoe or paddle to a teenager—unless, of course, you have to, because he or she belongs to you.

45.   Encourage a child to paddle a small
       canoe alone.

46.   Give a kid a canoe paddle that's sized to
       fit. Paint his or her name and date on
       the blade. This treasured item will be
       kept forever.

47. Choose a canoe pack that won't come apart when you lift it by a strap or buckle. When you're sure it's "tough enough," <u>then</u> try it on for comfort.

48. You won't lose gear on a wilderness canoe trip if each person always packs, and portages, the same items.

49. Everything should be multifunctional on a canoe trip. For example, the belly section of a three-piece fabric canoe cover may be used as a sail, tablecloth, windbreak or shelter for firewood.

50. Make a fabric splash cover for your wilderness tripping canoe. A cover keeps things dry in rain and rapids and cuts wind resistance by half or more! My book, *Canoeing Wild Rivers,* has plans for several models.

51. A canoe that's fitted with a nylon splash cover is only "marginally" safer in rapids than an open canoe. Remember this before you decide to "cover up and run" a drop you know you should have portaged!

52. You'll see the river more clearly if you color the eye panel of your insect head-net black (a magic marker or black spray paint works well).

53.   The backcountry would be a better place if everyone learned to tie quick-release knots.

54.   Every canoeist should know how to tie a *sheetbend, double half-hitch, bowline* and *power-cinch* (trucker's hitch). Enthusiasts will also learn the *double sheetbend* and *fisherman's knot*—plus, quick-release versions of them all.

55. When an icy wind comes up, you'll be glad you have a life jacket that's long enough to cover your kidneys.

56. God doesn't care how you paddle,
And neither do your friends.
So embrace what pleases you,
No need to make amends.

57. Leave beer at home where it can keep its cool.

58. Give your knees the support they deserve: glue closed-cell foam pads into your canoe. Waterproof contact cement never lets go.

59. Respect the wild in wilderness.

60. If you're canoeing in dangerous bear country, carry a can of ten percent pepper spray in a holster on your hip.

61. Portages go easier if you stack gear in the hollow of your back, and pack with a tumpline.

62. Adjust your tumpline before you begin a portage and you won't make tortured remarks.

63. If you portage two packs at once, carry them both on your back with the aid of a tumpline. *Don't* carry anything on your chest that prevents you from seeing your feet or the portage trail!

64. Get a thwart bag that doubles as a fanny
     pack or shoulder bag.

65. An auto mechanic is the most important
     person on a canoe expedition.

66. Wear your waterproof camera inside
     your life vest so it won't pendulum
     back and forth as you paddle. *Caution:*
     see #141!

67. You can define a canoeing "expert" in a single word: details!

68. Don't paddle stern (or bow) all the time!

69. Learn to turn your solo canoe by pulling the bow towards your paddle. This technique is far more effective than pushing the stern away.

70.   "Sleep tandem, paddle solo."

Tom Foster,
Former Chair of the ACA National Instruction
Committee, and author of
Catch Every Eddy, Surf Every Wave.

71. Canoeing alone is never lonely if all your friends have solo canoes.

72. It takes a while to become a proficient solo canoeist. Don't give up on the grand idea if you don't "get it" in the first season!

73. Shy away from any partner who says, "I've never tipped over!"

74. Don't let anyone talk you into paddling a rapid that's beyond your ability.

75. Don't get mad if you get stuck on a rock in the middle of a rapid. Instead, do the "attitude" stroke (twirl your paddle above your head, and <u>smile</u>!). This tells onlookers that you planned the event and you're right where you want to be!

– Dave Dietrich

76. Don't mix testosterone and whitewater.

77. Which canoe is "best for what" depends upon which car is best for what, which depends upon which truck is best for what. And don't forget how nice it is to travel by bus, train and plane.

78. No single canoe will do everything well. Those that claim to aren't much fun to paddle.

79.   Don't make such a fetish out of waterproofing your gear that you can't get to an aspirin, a chocolate bar or a good book.

80.   You can fit three seventeen-foot canoes inside a Dehaviland twin otter float plane if you remove two of the yokes and stack the canoes. Teach this trick to your pilot and you won't have to charter another flight.

81. Not all bush pilots are expert at tying canoes on float planes. Your pilot will be forever grateful if you teach him how to tie a "power cinch" (trucker's hitch).

82. Check the hubs of your canoe trailer every time you stop for gas. If hubs feel hot, pull the wheels and grease the bearings before you drive another mile.

83.   The long tongue is usually the first thing that breaks on a canoe trailer—often while you're cruising at freeway speeds. Check for stress cracks every time you stop for gas. Don't secure electrical wires to the tongue with wide tape that could mask hairline fractures.

84.   Shock absorbers will eliminate most of the vibration which is associated with the failure of canoe trailer components.

85.   Walk noisily in groups of four or more when portaging through grizzly country.

86.   Keels are almost always the mark of an inferior canoe.

87. Bring food and water on every canoe trip—even those that last only a few hours.

– Lynn Dietrich

88.　　The "four C's" of responsible wilderness canoe travel are *caution, commitment, caring* and *courage.*

　　　　　– Dr. Tom Schwinghamer

89.　　Don't be afraid to be afraid. Fear is nature's way of telling mature minds to think before they act.

90.   Why canoe wild rivers?
      The first time you startle a moose that's
      feeding quietly among the lily pads,
      silhouette emblazoned against a
      backdrop of new-born sun and morning
      mist, or watch ten thousand caribou do
      a thunder dance across the endless
      tundra, you'll know.

      From *Canoeing Wild Rivers,*
      by Cliff Jacobson

91. Inexpensive Tingley™ rubber over-shoes are light, flexible and 100 percent waterproof. They stick to wet rocks better than most wet shoes that are built for the purpose.

92. Outfit your car with an 80 inch wide rack that will carry two canoes.

93. Never allow a good canoe to be transported on a vehicle that does not have padded canoe racks.

94. Keep some scrap carpeting and duct tape in your car in the event you have to shuttle your canoe on someone else's unpadded racks.

95. Never store a wood-trimmed canoe outdoors, or lend it to anyone who is not a canoeing fanatic.

96. Don't allow anyone other than yourself or a canoeing fanatic, whose knots you trust, tie your canoe on a car or trailer.

97.   Keep your rain suit handy in case you have to portage through stinging nettles and poison ivy.

– Lynn Dietrich

98.   "You can learn to turn a fast canoe. But no amount of learning will make a slow canoe fast."

– Harry Roberts
Past editor of *Wilderness Camping* magazine and guru of "sit'n switch" style paddling.

99.   "When you're up to your neck in alligators it's hard to remember you came to drain the swamp!"

Translation: There's no time to think about how to turn a fast canoe when you're in the middle of a bad rapid. If you paddle whitewater, get a boat that turns. Rapidly!

– *Steve Scarborough*

Four time national whitewater champion and Vice President of Dagger Canoe Company.

100. If a canoe tracks like a mountain cat when empty, you'll need a winch to turn it when it's loaded. Translation: *Pack it like you'll use it, then try it before you buy it!*

101. A canoe can never be "too light!" And neither can a paddle.

102. Forty-two pounds is the kiss of death for a solo cruising canoe.

103. Don't buy any canoe you need help to carry.

104. Install loops of shock-cord through holes drilled in the thwarts of your canoe. The elastic organizes small items and keeps them put in wind.

105. Every sailor knows that loose lines and a rough sea don't mix. Coil your ropes and store them under loops of shock-cord on the decks of your canoe.

106. Three-eighths inch diameter Dacron sailing (sheet) line, and mantle-core "rescue-bag grade" polypropylene is the best rope for lining a canoe.

107. Carry a large natural sponge. It's much more absorbent than a synthetic sponge, and it adds a splash of elegance to your canoe.

108. Cut off the bottom of a plastic bleach jug and you'll have an efficient bailer for your canoe.

109.   If you paddle a wood-trimmed canoe on an icy day, dry the floor *before you turn it over* and put it away!

The idea is to prevent bilge water from soaking into the decks and rails where it may freeze and cause the wood to warp. "Putting 'em away wet" may be why some Royalex canoes crack in cold weather.

110. Two skinny bolts are better than one fat one. Remember this when you attach yokes and thwarts to your canoe.

111. Paddle at sunrise and sunset with someone you love.

112. Trust your bow paddler!

113. Gender equality is paddling your own solo canoe.

114. Wash your canoe after every trip. Wax it once a season.

115. You'll kneel more comfortably if the front edge of your seat is one-half inch lower than the back.

116. A foam padded seat makes for a hot duff.

117. Raise your canoe seat if you want more comfort and power. Lower it, if you want more stability.

118. The most important thing on a canoe trip is a dry pair of socks.

119. The most frivolous thing on a canoe trip is a partner who won't stop talking.

120. Bring two head nets if you're canoeing in Canada in June.

121. An insulated mug beats a steel Sierra cup any time.

122. Slow down your pace and wait for your friends. They want to see—not hear about—the wildlife you just saw!

123. Stay at least fifty feet away from a cow moose and calf.

124. If you canoe within snorting distance of a rutting bull moose, reverse engines and pray!

125. If a curious polar bear follows your canoe across the river, power to the other side; then power back to the other side; then power back to the other side!

126. If a black bear cub appears to follow your canoe, change directions or stop paddling. The frightened youngster is probably swimming towards its mother who is waiting on shore.

127. Go on an overnight canoe trip with your fiancee. If you're still talking to one another the next day, you'll probably enjoy a successful marriage.

– Lynn Dietrich

128. It takes more than a decade to grow a ten-pound Arctic lake trout. Remember this before you make a meal of him.

129. Catch-and-release fishing is just a catchword if you don't use barbless hooks.

130. Serious canoeing and fishing mix. Serious fishing and canoeing don't.

131. Bring a hard case for your fishing rods.

132. The bottom of an inverted canoe makes a handy table.

133. Bury fish remains 150 feet from water, well away from camp. Don't throw entrails in the water unless there are grizzly bears about.

134. If you come upon fish entrails at the base of a rapid along an Arctic river, skedaddle fast. A grizzly bear <u>is</u> nearby!

135. If you meet a polar bear along an Arctic river, remember that he can swim around five miles an hour. That's faster than you can paddle your canoe!

136. Don't limit your canoeing to far away places. Discover the beauty and challenge of nearby waters.

137. Learn to read a tide table if you paddle the rivers near Labrador and Hudson's Bay. And remember to convert values to local time!

138. A small battery-operated GPS is a comforting thing to have along if you canoe complex lakes and deltas.

139. Carry three compasses on a wilderness canoe trip: a small Orienteering model that will fit in your pocket; a larger instrument for precision course plotting, and a tough glow-in-the-dark diving compass to strap around a thwart. You've probably been out too long if all three begin to argue with one another.

140. Don't put monkey fists, loops or knots of any kind on the end of lining ropes or lanyards. They may catch on something if you capsize.

141. Don't paddle rapids while wearing anything on a cord around your neck.

142. Keep bug dope, hand cream and sun-tan lotion in a small zippered thwart bag where you can reach them.

143. The quickest way to become a good paddler is to buy a solo canoe.

144. Don't let a flatwater racer or freestyle paddler tell you what kind of canoe to buy for wilderness tripping. Seek advice from experts who've lived your dreams.

145. Make it known throughout the land that you will not lend canoes or camping gear to anyone who is not a rabid canoeist.

146. If you need canoes for a teen trip, rent them or buy them. If you want real sorrow, borrow!

147. Pounce on puppy love before a canoe trip. Ask google-eyed teens to draw a sociogram that indicates their friends, acquaintances and enemies. *Acquaintances* of the opposite sex are often madly in love!

148. The rule for canoeing with teens is, work 'em hard, feed 'em well, and program all their time.

149. If you don't keep kids busy on a canoe trip they'll begin to act like "normal" children.

150. The best blend on any canoe trip is an equal mix of boys and girls or men and women.

151. Teenagers go canoeing largely to be with their friends. Remember this before you invite their parents.

152. An adult canoe trip is an introspective event. It is no place for children.

153. You can't out-paddle a rapid, but you can out-think it.

154. Take the scouting out of a whitewater outing and you may have to swim home!

155. Get on the level with the river. Rapids look much larger when viewed from above.

156. Odd gets the nod when it's time to portage. One, three or five packs are better than two or four.

157. Two packs—one heavy, one light—will balance a solo canoe just right.

158. Don't bring more stuff than <u>you</u> are willing to carry.

159. Light makes right. Sixty-five pounds per person is a fashionable load for a one-week canoe trip. Add about 15 pounds for every extra week you're out.

160. Keep your paddle in a protective "paddle bag" while you're on the road. You can buy paddle bags at any canoe shop, or simply sew your own.

161. Your "draw" stroke will be much more powerful if you use an aerial, rather than an underwater recovery.

162. If you can't run the rapid, line around it; if you can't line, portage; if you can't portage, unload your boat and haul it over the rocks, up the canyon or through the woods. If these are all impossible, check your GPS: you're probably on the wrong planet!

163. When in doubt, portage!

164. The trip leader is a little bit mother, a little more example, a source of knowledge, and the great anticipator.
    – *Mike Link*

165. A dam site is no place for a canoe!

166. Don't practice upstream ferries above a falls.

167. Tie up your canoe whenever you go ashore.

168. It's a gracious act to share your campsite with another canoe party—especially, if it's late in the day and you have the only show in town.

169. Life jackets are life-saving equipment. Don't stuff them into a pack, sit on them or leave them out in the rain.

170. It is the duty of *canoeists* to politely remind canoers that they should wear their life jackets.

171. Get a life jacket that's long enough to cover your kidneys. You'll appreciate its warmth in a following wind, and its padding if you have to swim a rocky rapid on your back.

172. "Always wear your life jacket on an icy Arctic river. It makes the bodies easier to find."

– Bob O'Hara
Bob O'Hara has canoed most of the rivers in the central Arctic.

173. Why is it that some people will pay a premium price for a lightweight canoe then tie ten pounds of gear on it when they portage?

174. Wooden canoe paddles may warp if stored for very long in a horizontal postion. Most canoeists just hang them from cord or pegs.

175. If you're trying to hitch a ride back to your car after a canoe trip, carry a canoe paddle. Then, you'll look like a canoeist rather than a bum.

176. If you want to go fast without a lot of work, use a double-bladed paddle in your solo canoe.

177. "Real" canoeists leave their canoe racks on their cars all winter!

178. Thompson's Water Seal® is great for waterproofing maps, journals and tent seams. Most hardware stores have it.

179. Don't take maps too seriously. Read the river. And believe it!

180. Learn the metric system if you canoe in Canada.

181. Give your charter float plane pilot something to remember you by. A six pack of American beer or a fifth of Yankee bourbon is a polite tradition.

182. This rule suggests on which side of a river bend your canoe should be. High water—bend inside; low water—bend outside. Otherwise, enjoy a little of the middle.

183. If you capsize, stay <u>upstream</u> of your canoe. Pinned between a swamped canoe and a rock is a hard place to be.

184. Don't stand in a current that's strong. If a foot becomes trapped between rocks, you won't last long!

185. If you capsize in a rapid, roll on your back, toes up and pointed downstream. Your life jacket will support you as you "ride 'em downstream, cowboy!"

186. First, carry your gear over the portage and familiarize yourself with the route. *Then*, bring the canoe.

187. After you've carried all *your* gear to the end of the portage, go back and help your friends. Then go back and help their friends and their friends and their friends…

188. Canoes have the right-of-way over power boats. Wise paddlers won't press the issue.

189. If a power boat approaches you at breakneck speed, flash a huge smile and a big thumbs down. Captain Nemo will probably get the cue and throttle back.

190. Your aluminum canoe will slide over rocks—rather than stick to them—if you apply a thick coat of paste wax to the hull. No need to buff the wax.

191. Paint the decks of your aluminum canoe flat black to reduce glare.

192. Paint will stick better to an aluminum canoe if you wash it with vinegar before you paint it.

193. Whenever you wash or capsize your canoe, the foam-filled yoke pads absorb water like a sponge and drip for days. Drill some holes in the wood yoke pad blocks so water can get out fast.

194. Use only brass, bronze or stainless steel hardware on canoes and canoe covers. A magnet or compass needle will reveal the nature of the metal.

195. The Minnesota Canoe Association is
      the largest recreational canoe club—
      and the largest canoe building club—in
      the world. The MCA has plans for
      more than a dozen canoe models, plus
      the best wood-strip canoe building
      manual. If you plan to build a stripper,
      join the MCA!

196. The hardest thing about building a
wood-strip canoe is making the
strongback and forms. No need to go
to the trouble if you belong to the
MCA. You'll find forms for rent and
forms for sale. Some builders will give
you their old forms just to create space
in their garage.

197. Don't shy away from buying a wood-strip canoe. Strippers are very light, easy to repair, and much stronger than most people believe. But, they depreciate rapidly—which is to your advantage if you want to buy a used one.

198. Wooden canoes are magic: ever notice how people always touch them when they walk by?

199. It is neither macho nor "macha" to wear a thread-bare life jacket. It is downright foolish! Replace your PFD *before* it wears out!

– Lynn Dietrich

200. Concerned about a particular rapid? Ask the locals, but don't take their advice too seriously. Most don't understand canoes, or canoeists.

201. Women who canoe in bug country may want to discover the Sani-Fem® discreet urination device.

202. Buy canoes in the fall; sell them in the spring.

203. The location of canoe seats and thwarts is not ordained by God. If you don't like how your boat's set up, change it!

204. Canoes run best when they are trimmed dead level. Some enthusiasts epoxy a small fish-eye bubble into the hull; others pour a cup of water onto the floor and see which way it flows.

205. If your canoe doesn't have a sliding
bow seat, use this formula to determine
where the seats should be:

$$\frac{\text{BOW PERSON'S WEIGHT}}{\text{DISTANCE FROM BOW}} = \frac{\text{STERN PERSON'S WEIGHT}}{\text{(UNKNOWN) DISTANCE FROM STERN}}$$

or more simply:

$$\text{DISTANCE FROM STERN} = \frac{\text{STERN PERSON'S WEIGHT X DISTANCE FROM THE BOW}}{\text{BOW PERSON'S WEIGHT}}$$

206. Drill some holes through plastic and aluminum canoe seats so they won't pool water when it rains.

207. Cane seats will last longer if you occasionally oil them with Watco® or Djeks Olay®. Varnish dries out cane and makes it brittle.

208. Choose brightly colored canoes and gear if you're going to the barrenlands. Your float plane pilot won't find you if you blend in with the environment.

209. Review your map scale before you cross a wide bay on a barrenlands lake. What looks like a few hundred yards is often a mile or more!

210. Know how to rescue a swamped canoe, and carry the rope and hardware to do it.

211. If you want the best deal on a good used canoe, buy it from someone who knows and loves canoeing. Enthusiasts will accentuate the positives and exaggerate the negatives, even if it means losing a sale. Honest!

212. Ultra-violet light quickly kills canoes. If you must store a wood or plastic canoe in the blazing sun, apply a UV inhibitor to the hull and trim. Your local marina will help you find what you need.

213. Don't store a wood or plastic canoe near a garage window where the sun can shine on it. Read #212 and you'll see why.

214. Every auto buff knows better than to cover a car with non-porous nylon or plastic to protect it from the weather. Canoeists should know it too!

215. Two or three canoe lengths off shore may be the safest place to be in a lightning storm. That's because a lightning-protected zone extends from the tops of the tallest trees (or other topographic features) outward about 45 degrees in all directions.

216. Don't run rapids with three in a canoe!

217. If you capsize, stay with your canoe *only* if doing so won't endanger your life!

218.   It takes courage to cancel a canoe trip down a river which has been flooded by a recent rain, especially if you've planned the event for weeks. But the river will be there later in the season—and if you make the right decision—so will you!

219. You can never have too much toilet paper on a canoe trip.

220. If possible, always set packsacks upright in a canoe. This keeps the mouths of their waterproof liners from being submerged in bilge water.

221. Most canoe packs have closing flaps that are too short. Matching fabric and a sewing machine will make things right.

222. Leave your radio at home; the river has its own music.

223. Waterproof binoculars are wonderful!

224. Make a profile of any wilderness river you plan to paddle. A drop of five feet per mile is nice cruising; fifteen means a probable portage. And twenty-five is about the limit of a loaded open canoe.

225.   Remember these map-reading tricks:

1.   The larger the Contour Interval, the less you can tell about the river.

2.   The closed or "vee" end of a contour line always points *upstream.*

3.   Where contour lines cross or run very close together, you'll find an abrupt drop—a falls or canyon.

226. Portages, rest stops, meals and scouting rapids take time. Two miles an hour is an average pace on a wilderness canoe trip.

227. Fifteen miles a day is a reasonable goal on a wilderness canoe trip.

228.   Make a time and distance schedule for any wild river you plan to canoe. And be where you're supposed to be when you're supposed to be! Leave a copy of your schedule with your friends back home, so they'll know when you're supposed to be where.

229. When you plan your time and distance schedule, allow one day in five as lost time due to wind and bad weather.

230. Don't buy any canoe until you've paddled it!

– Betty Ketter

231. Marry someone who loves canoeing.

232. Take canoe field-tests done by industry magazines with a grain of salt. Add pepper if all the testing was performed by a single person in a single day.

233. Any canoe is better than no canoe!

234. Wind some duct tape around a canoe thwart. Wind some more around another thwart. Carry what remains of the roll in your pack.

235. Give someone who loves canoeing a canoe book for Christmas.

236. If you want a good buy on a lean, fast canoe, attend a canoe race. Find the last place loser and make a low ball offer he or she can't refuse.

237. You won't find good canoes advertised in newspapers.

238. Sweethearts who paddle solo canoes
      may glide side-by-side and steal a kiss.
      Sweethearts who paddle tandem canoes
      must go ashore to steal a kiss.

239. Always lean *downstream*!

              – *Dave Dietrich*

240. Bright colors are hot and olive drab ones are not when you're portaging through knee-high tag alder in the middle of nowhere. If you flag your packs, and the trail, with pink plastic surveying tape, you won't lose your gear or your way.

– Sue Harings

241. Wood-canvas canoes never die; they just accumulate new parts.

242. If you don't want to scratch your new canoe, keep it garaged.

243. Put it on plastic to ensure a fair rate of foreign exchange in Canada. Everything from float plane fare to gas purchases can be put on VISA.

244. Don't leave your billfold and keys in your car while you're canoeing!

245. If you carry your car keys in a pocket while you're canoeing, tether them to your belt with a piece of parachute cord.

246. Don't follow another canoe too closely through rapids.

247. Don't walk too closely behind a canoe that's being portaged. If the canoe stops quick, you could get a fractured face!

– Sue Harings

248. Kids need good canoe shoes too. Low cut sneakers and rubber overshoes (galoshes or slip-ons) keep feet dry in any weather.

249. If you're camped along a barrenlands river and there's no place to tie your canoe, leave the craft right-side-up and set some heavy packs inside. Then, snap on the fabric splash cover so rain can't get in.

250. Don't wear thick-soled mountaineering boots in a canoe unless you plan to climb the river.

251. You can't have too many tubes of lip gloss on a canoe trip.

252. Paper toweling has many uses on a canoe trip. Why not splurge and bring a roll?

253. *Polarized* sunglasses enable you to see the rocks in rapids. Bow paddlers may want to keep this a secret so their stern partners won't blame them when they mess up.

254.   A Leatherman®, Gerber Multipliers® or other multi-purpose tool is essential equipment on all canoe trips.

255.   A pile neck-warmer, balaclava and knitted wristlets take the chill out of cold weather canoeing.

– Sue Harings

256. If you go canoeing in Minnesota around Christmas, you'll want to wear double wool socks and felt snowmobile liners inside Tingley® rubber overshoes. You can probably eliminate one pair of socks if you take advantage of the January thaw.

257. Don't take for granted a river you've paddled many times before. High water, low water or blow downs that produce "strainers," can turn a placid route into a death-defying run. If in doubt, get out and scout!

258. Clean up your canoeing and camping gear as soon as you return home from a trip.

259. Don't put all your food in one packsack—Charles Atlas could get a hernia.

260. It is safe to put all your eggs in one pack basket—that is, if you have a cover for it. Tip: Duluth Tent and Awning, Inc. (Duluth, Minnesota) makes a special "Cruiser" pack that will accept an 18-inch high pack basket.

261. Practice makes perfect only if you do things right all the time!

262. Don't tie objects to canoe seats or strap packs under seats. Anything which interferes with kneeling could trap your feet in a capsize.

263. Keep some eyeglass cleaning solution and a clean, cotton handkerchief in a Zip-lock bag in your thwart bag.

264.   Unless you have an experienced partner and a straight-tracking canoe, you're better off to paddle *straight into* big waves than to quarter (angle into) them.

265.   Lighten *both* ends of your canoe when you run big rapids without a splash cover. The simplest solution is for both partners to move closer to the yoke.

266.   Level the canoe or trim the downstream end *slightly* down before you ferry across a strong current.

267. Bury uneaten food 150 feet from water.

268. Toilet paper will decompose more quickly if you burn it before you bury it. Carry a water bottle and make sure the fire is dead out!

269. Don't bring glass bottles on a canoe trip.

270. The "string pull method" is the most painless way to remove a fish-hook that's embedded in the skin. It's illustrated in Dr. Forgey's book, *Wilderness Medicine, 4th Edition.*

271. If you must canoe across an expanse of open water, go in the evening when the wind is down, not at dawn just before it comes up.

272. A marine "orange smoke" bomb, with 50 second burning time, is the most visible daylight distress signal you can carry on a wilderness canoe trip.

273. Don't pack all your emergency signalling equipment in one canoe.

274. Practice paddling backwards. When you can maintain a straight course, and go right and left without missing a beat, you're ready for the river.

275. If you wreck your canoe on a remote river and fear you will have to be rescued by air, move your camp to a deep water area where a float plane can land.

276. If you're canoeing in Canada, register your canoe trip with the Royal Canadian Mounted Police. And be sure to "de-register" as soon as you're off the water!

277. A candle lantern and a good book will light your tent and warm your heart.

278.   An aerial photo is the best way to locate a route around dangerous water, without actually being there. Both the U.S. and Canadian governments have extensive air photo files. Some photos are available in "stereo pairs."

279.   Mark your canoe route (and all rapids) on your topographic map with a brightly colored "highlighter," like that which students use to emphasize their notes.

280. Order *Land Use Information Series* maps if you're canoeing in northern Canada. They are standard 1:250,000 scale topo maps that are over-printed with information about wildlife, vegetation, geology and climate.

281. Remember to change meters to feet when you determine the drop per mile of a Canadian river!

282.   Use this rhyme to adjust your compass for area magnetic declination:

- *Declination east, compass least*: **Subtract** the value of the declination from your true map bearing.

- *Declination west, compass best*: **Add** the value of the declination to your true map bearing.

283. Don't store your compass in a metal desk or drawer: It may reverse its polarity!

284. Bring a wooden pencil and waterproof notebook on every canoe trip.

285. Order your raincoat at least one size larger than you think you need. Alter the collar so it will seal tightly around your neck.

286. A Thermos bottle saves many times its weight in the fuel needed to heat water.

287. A dip in the horizon usually indicates the outlet of a lake or channel.

288. Nylon packs and tents may not rot if you store them in a damp basement, but the waterproof coatings and cotton-polyester stitching will!

289. Plastic trash-compactor bags make tough, waterproof liners for packsacks.

290. An industrial supply store is a good place to shop for outdoor gear. Tingley® rubber boots, lightweight rain gear, Kevlar fishing gloves and giant (36" x 60") six-mil thick plastic bags are among the useful things you'll find.

291. Carry a tape recorder and capture the sounds of the river.

292. A money belt is a more secure place for dollars than a packsack.

293. Don't buy a sleeping bag that's built for winter unless this is your usual canoeing time.

294.   Spend your money on things you use every day on a canoe trip, not on frills which sometimes come in handy.

295.   You need three hats on a canoe trip— one for rain, one for warmth, and one for "style."

296. A plastic pink flamingo or an inflatable orange octopus is worth bringing on a canoe trip, if it makes you smile.

297. A cap for your cup keeps mosquitoes out of the cocoa.

298. Don't place a plastic canoe too near a campfire.

299. Here's a reliable way to waterproof your sleeping bag:
   1. Stuff the bag into a nylon sack which need not be waterproof.
   2. Place the nylon sack into a plastic trash compactor bag. Seal the bag with a rubber band.
   3. Nest this unit inside an oversize nylon stuff sack, which need not be waterproof. Note that the plastic bag is sandwiched between two layers of strong nylon.

300. If you pack long tent poles under the closing flap of a pack, tie the pole bag (sew on security loops) to a strap or buckle so the poles can't slide out.

301. If you need quick shelter in a vertical rain, prop up one end of your canoe on poles or paddles. Or, just rest the bow on the limb of a tree.

302. Padded bicycle shorts take the edge off a hard canoe seat.

303. Learn these universal paddling signals—STOP, HELP/EMERGENCY and ALL CLEAR.

304. Learn to pole your canoe so you can go up a creek without a paddle.

305. Be an environmental watch-dog. Document (photograph!) and report pollution problems every place you paddle.

306. Watch out for barbed wire fences which cross small rivers!

307. Tag barbed wire fences with brightly-colored surveying tape so other canoeists won't run into them.

308. Don't canoe a trout stream on the opening day of fishing season!

309. Don't bury the hatchet; a small axe is very useful on a canoe trip.

310. *Don't* use rubber ropes or elastic bungee cords to tie your canoe on a car!

311. An ice chest is a convenient dry box for river trips. Duct tape will make it rapids proof.

312. Never "bridge" a canoe—that is, climb aboard it when it's half on land and half on water.

313. You won't get turned around in a river if you remember these current landing rules: Beach your canoe *stern* first (backferry ashore) when going downstream. Beach *bow* first (forward ferry ashore) when going upstream.

314. Master these maneuvers before you canoe a dangerous river: backferry, forward ferry, side-slip, eddy turn, peel-out. Add good judgment and everyone will return alive.

315.   Incompetence spawns scary adventures.
       Knowledge and judgment make
       memorable experiences.

Inspired by the great Arctic explorer
– *Vihjalmur Steffanson*

316. Learn to tack your canoe across a windy bay. A sailing manual will show you how.

317. Canoeing in wind is a breeze if you trim the hull bow down (one inch is enough) when beating up-wind, and stern down when running down-wind.

318. If you want an upsetting experience, paddle your tandem canoe alone from the stern seat!

319. The proper place to solo a tandem canoe is at or near the middle. On *quiet* water, you may sit backwards on the bow seat and make the stern the bow.

320. Check for dew on the bottom of an overturned canoe before you retire for the night. If the bottom's wet, you can bet there is no rain in sight.

321. Rig a rain-fly in camp every night, even when there is dew on the bottom of your canoe.

322. Create your own adventure. Pack your maps away and read the river for a day.

323. Fresh fruits and vegetables won't bruise on a canoe trip if you pack them inside a coffee pot or tea kettle.

324. Everyone on a canoe trip should have a specific job assignment—cook, cook's helper, fire-tender, dish-washer, gopher, etc. Rotate work assignments every few days.

325. Six people (three canoes) is the ideal size for a canoe expedition. Here's why:

1. If one canoe is wrecked, the crew can crowd into the remaining boats.
2. Six people and three canoes will fit in the belly of a twin otter float plane, which is usually the cheapest way to fly.
3. Six hands are strong enough to lift a loaded canoe over the meanest obstacles.

326. Canoes should show some battle scars.
      Shows you're a canoeist not a canoer!

– Bob Brown
Bob Brown has designed canoes for Bell,
Blackhawk, Mad-River,
Old Town and We-no-nah.

327. Learn to lean your canoe to make gradual turns. Lean left to turn right, and right to turn left: it's the opposite of taking a curve on a bicycle.

328. Paddle a light canoe that makes you smile, even if it develops holes after awhile.

329. Learn to judge the performance of a canoe by the sound of its wake. Swift, lean hulls make quiet hissing sounds; inefficient craft gurgle like percolating coffee grounds.

330. It's okay to stand in a canoe. In fact, it's the best way to get a clear view of the rapid you are about to run. Caution: Never allow *standing and looking* to take the place of *walking and scouting*!

331. Bring Robert Service on a canoe trip. Stoke the campfire to a crackling glow, then launch *The Cremation of Sam McGee*.

332. These classic canoe books will bring you joy: *Canoeing With The Cree, Lure of the Labrador Wild, Rushton and His Times In American Canoeing, Bark and Skin Boats of North America and North American Canoe Country.*

333. Learn how to play *Dead fish polo* and *Duct tape tag*.

– Charlie Wilson
Charlie is a national Freestyle canoe champion and Vice President of Bell Canoe Works.

334. Man is a gregarious being. Yet his most profound moments generally occur when he is alone.

– Calvin Rutstrum
(professing the joy of solo canoeing).

335. No one likes a mile bagger or a river bagger or a rapids bagger.

336. Wear your life jacket, even if your friends don't.

337. It takes years to develop the proper respect for a dangerous river. Don't rush it by doing something stupid.

338. Stop and make hot soup before a chilling death sets in.

339. Learn the "canoe-over-canoe" rescue.

340. If you want to avoid danger, forget all advice about "being careful." Focus instead on learning how to paddle well!

341. Don't pick a canoe on the strength of its material. Ship shape is everything!

342. Have you noticed that the best canoeists often drive the worst cars? Get yourself a beater if you want to fit in.

343. The best canoes are those you build yourself.

344. If you don't have space enough to build a full sized canoe, make a scale model. There are some great wood-strip kits available.

345. Canoe building is a winter event. Summer, spring and fall are the time for paddling.

346. Learn how to make eddy turns so you don't always have to go with the flow.

347. Before you commit to running a rapid, first discuss "where and how?" Then ask "what if?"

348. Unless it's an antique, the age of a canoe does not affect its resale value. Quality of design and material condition are all that matter.

349. Try to paddle the most difficult rapids in someone else's canoe!

– Darrell Foss

350. If you want a good deal on a well-used canoe, find one that looks that way. Then, learn how to repair it.

351. New stuff is nice but it's not necessarily best.

352. A canoe expedition is no place to test new or unfamiliar gear.

353. Don't judge the performance of a canoe until you've used it for a year.

354. Poor rain gear fails during the first storm. Good stuff lasts two or three seasons. Foul weather sailing suits that have double knees and double seats keep you dry almost forever.

355. Don't wear navy blue clothes or rain gear. Mosquitoes and black flies love the color!

356. There's more joy in paddling a bad canoe with a good paddle than vice versa.

357. Efficiency is the mother of tradition.

358. Break tradition if it brings you joy.

359. Canoeing is like dancing; timing is everything.

360. Tense paddling is tight and tiring; relaxed paddling is smooth and flowing.

– The Minnesota Canoe Association

361. Learn these efficient paddling tips:
    1. Pick up the tempo; don't "muscle up" for power.
    2. Keep the paddle shaft as vertical as possible when you stroke.
    3. Use your torso, not your biceps, to move the boat.
    4. Cleanly slice the paddle blade into the water, then firmly "anchor" it before you pull.
        – The Minnesota Canoe Association

362. Learn the pitch stroke—it is the most powerful and efficient way to keep a canoe on course without changing paddle sides.

363. If you see uprooted weeds or floating logs in a river you are about to paddle, abort the trip immediately. Your river is in flood stage!

– Lynn Dietrich

364. If you own a tandem canoe and a solo
canoe, try to remember when you last
used the tandem?

365. Don't worry about getting scratches on
your new canoe. Chances are the boat
will outlive you.